Countries Around the World

South Korea

Elizabeth Raum

www.raintreepublishers.co.uk

Visit our website to find out
more information about
Raintree books.

To order:

☎ Phone 0845 6044371

🖹 Fax +44 (0) 1865 312263

🖥 Email myorders@raintreepublishers.co.uk

Customers from outside the UK please telephone +44 1865 312262

Raintree is an imprint of Capstone Global Library Limited,
a company incorporated in England and Wales having its
registered office at 7 Pilgrim Street, London, EC4V 6LB –
Registered company number: 6695582

Text © Capstone Global Library Limited 2012
First published in hardback in 2012
The moral rights of the proprietor have been asserted.

Edited by Abby Colich and Claire Throp
Designed by Ryan Frieson and Steven Mead
Original illustrations © Capstone Global Library Ltd, 2012
Illustrated by Oxford Designers & Illustrators
Picture research by Ruth Blair
Originated by Capstone Global Library Ltd
Printed in China by China Translation and Printing Services

ISBN 978 1 406 23551 7
15 14 13 12 11
10 9 8 7 6 5 4 3 2 1

British Library Cataloguing in Publication Data
Raum, Elizabeth.
South Korea. -- (Countries around the world)
951.9'505-dc22
A full catalogue record for this book is available from the British
Library.

Acknowledgements
We would like to thank the following for permission to
reproduce photographs: Corbis pp. 8 (© Kim Kyung-hoon/
Reuters), 9 (© Bettmann), 10 (© Nathan Benn), 12 (© YNA/
epa), 14 (© Philippe Lissac/GODONG), 18 (© Rungroj Yongrit/
epa), 20 (© Hussein Malla/POOL/epa), 21 (© Jo Yong-hak/
Reuters), 22 (© YONHAP/epa), 26 (© Atlantide Phototravel),
29 (© he lulu/Xinhua Press), 30 (© Michel Setboun); Getty
Images pp. 11 (Kim Ho-Young/Korea Pool), 28 (Stephen
Lovekin), 33 (Dennis Gottlieb/FoodPix), 35 (Park Yeong-cheol/
AFP); iStockphoto p. 25 (© leesungjae); Photolibrary pp. 6
(Fotosearch), 17 (Eric Baccega/Age footstock); Shutterstock pp.
5 (© Steve Rosset), 31 (© Olga Besnard), 38 (© Chen Wei Seng),
46 (© wavebreakmedia ltd).

Cover photograph of the Myeongdong shopping district in
Seoul, South Korea reproduced with permission of Corbis
(© Lo Mak/Redlink)

We would like to thank Jennifer Jung-Kim for her invaluable
help in the preparation of this book.

Every effort has been made to contact copyright holders of
any material reproduced in this book. Any omissions will
be rectified in subsequent printings if notice is given to the
publisher.

Disclaimer
All the Internet addresses (URLs) given in this book were valid
at the time of going to press. However, due to the dynamic
nature of the Internet, some addresses may have changed, or
sites may have changed or ceased to exist since publication.
While the author and Publishers regret any inconvenience this
may cause readers, no responsibility for any such changes can be
accepted by either the author or the Publishers.

Note on Romanization of Korean
McCune-Reischauer is the Romanization method preferred
by academics. This is a phonetic system that reflects Korean
pronunciation. But some people find this system difficult because
it takes time to learn.

Since 2000, the South Korean government has been using a
different system that is easier to learn. North Korea uses yet another
method of Romanization that also has numerous exceptions, but it
is not used in this book except where the name or term is commonly
known in the West (for example, Kim Il Sung, Kim Jong Il, Juche).

This book primarily uses the South Korean system except when
names are more commonly spelled in a different way (for example,
Syngman Rhee and Kim Il Sung). The McCune-Reischauer system is
given in parentheses after the first use of the South Korean system.

Contents

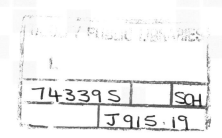
Some words in the book are in bold, **like this**. You can find out what they mean by looking in the glossary.

Introducing South Korea

South Korea is a land of contrasts. Modern South Korean companies make cars, ships, computers, and wireless communication systems. Millions of people live in high-rise buildings in clean, modern cities. Seoul, South Korea's capital, is a safe and attractive place for people to live. In 2010, it was named the World Design Capital.

Visitors can see modern buildings and ancient temples on the same tour. South Koreans preserve ancient **shrines** and temples. These very old buildings provide a look into Korea's past life and **culture**. Many South Koreans wear traditional clothing for special occasions. They also hold ceremonies to honour their **ancestors**. South Koreans respect their past, while working to create an even better future.

Where is South Korea?

South Korea is officially called the **Republic** of Korea. It occupies the southern half of the Korean **Peninsula**. It is located between the Yellow Sea and the East Sea. The East Sea extends along the southern coast of South Korea. An **artificial** boundary called the **Demilitarized Zone (DMZ)** separates South Korea from its neighbouring country, North Korea. South Korea has a total area of 99,720 square kilometres (38,502 square miles). That is about the same size as Scotland and Wales.

Daily Life

Koreans greet one another with a quick, short bow. The bow is often a nodding of the head. Young people bow to their parents, teachers, and employers. Bowing is a sign of respect.

This is one of the traditional
temples that can be found in Seoul.

History: a land divided

Stone Age people lived on the Korean **Peninsula** about 40,000 years ago. Today's Koreans trace their **ancestors** to people who arrived from Manchuria, Mongolia, and southern Siberia between 8,000 and 3,000 BC. These people built villages, kept animals, and wove cloth. They made useful tools and weapons. They also built the first **dolmens**, which are burial tombs. Korea has more dolmens – 30,000 – than any other place in the world.

Korean kingdoms

Koreans believe their nation began in 2333 BC, when a leader called Dangun (also called Tan'gun) founded the Old Joseon (also called Choson) Kingdom. Old Joseon lasted for over 2,000 years. For the next several thousand years, various kingdoms ruled Korea. Each one introduced new ideas and customs.

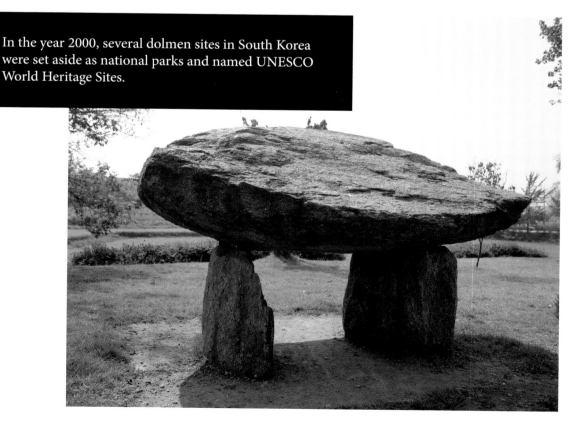

In the year 2000, several dolmen sites in South Korea were set aside as national parks and named UNESCO World Heritage Sites.

In 108 BC, China's Han **Dynasty** (206 BC–AD 220) conquered Old Joseon. The Han brought Chinese **culture** and customs to Korea. From AD 668 to 935, the entire Korean Peninsula came together under the rule of the later Silla Dynasty. Many people in the kingdom became **Buddhist**. Over 200 Buddhist temples were built during this time. Later, Silla grew weak over time, and the Goryeo (also called Koryo) Dynasty (918–1392) gained control. The English word "Korea" comes from the native Korean word *Goryeo*.

RUSSIA

CHINA

NORTH KOREA

Korea Bay

East Sea

■Pyongyang

Demilitarized zone (DMZ)

38°N

■Seoul

SOUTH KOREA

KOREAN PENINSULA

Yellow Sea

JAPAN

Korea Strait

Jeju Strait

Jeju

The Korean Peninsula (shown here in orange) has always been strongly influenced by China to the north and Japan to the east.

0   200 kilometres

0   100 miles

N

The Joseon Dynasty

In 1392, the Joseon Dynasty extended Korea's borders north. Hanyang (present-day Seoul) became the capital. Joseon leaders valued education and art. In 1377 they printed the first book in the world using moveable type. After repeated attacks and a war with Japan (1592–1598), Joseon rulers closed Korea's borders to outsiders. Korea became known as the Hermit Kingdom. (A hermit is someone who does not interact with the rest of the world.)

YI SUN-SIN (1545–1598)

Yi Sun-sin, one of Korea's greatest heroes, was a naval commander who built the world's first "ironclad" ships, which were ships covered in protective metal. Spikes covered these "turtle ships", and a dragon's head held a cannon in its mouth. Yi Sun-sin's forces defeated Japan in the 1500s.

Schoolchildren study this model of a turtle ship from the 1500s.

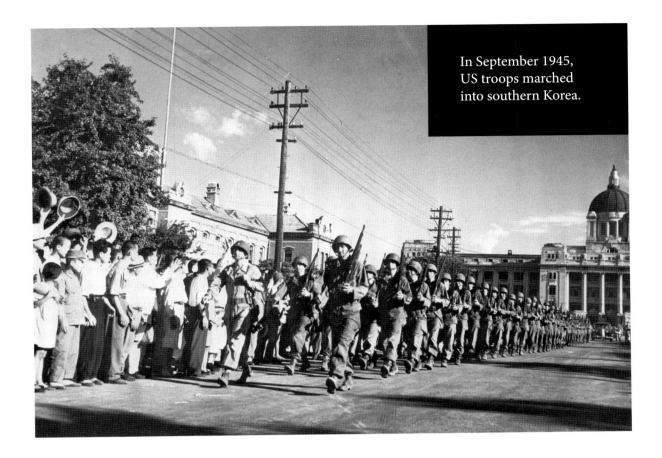

In September 1945, US troops marched into southern Korea.

A nation divided

In 1910 Japan made Korea a **colony** Japan remained in control of Korea until 1945, when World War II ended. Koreans celebrated Japan's defeat. Many Koreans had suffered under Japanese rule. Now they wanted to become independent.

Korea's neighbour, the **Soviet Union**, had worked to defeat Japan. The United States had worked with the Soviet Union. However, the Soviet Union was a **communist** country. The United States did not want Korea to become communist, too. So from 10 to 11 August 1945, US officials split Korea in half. Troops from the Soviet Union moved into northern Korea. US troops moved into southern Korea.

The Korean War (1950–1953)

On 15 August 1948, South Korea became a **democracy**. Syngman Rhee, the first president, was a Korean educated in the United States. Meanwhile, neighbouring North Korea became communist. Both countries began plotting a takeover of each other. North Korea moved first.

On 25 June 1950, North Korean troops crossed into South Korea. They overpowered the poorly trained South Korean army and conquered Seoul. The **United Nations (UN)** sent troops from 16 countries to support South Korea. China and the Soviet Union supported North Korea. Almost 3 million people died before fighting ended on 27 July 1953. North Korea and the United States agreed to stop the fighting and create a **Demilitarized Zone (DMZ)** between the two countries, to keep fighting forces separate. The DMZ also forms the border between the two Koreas.

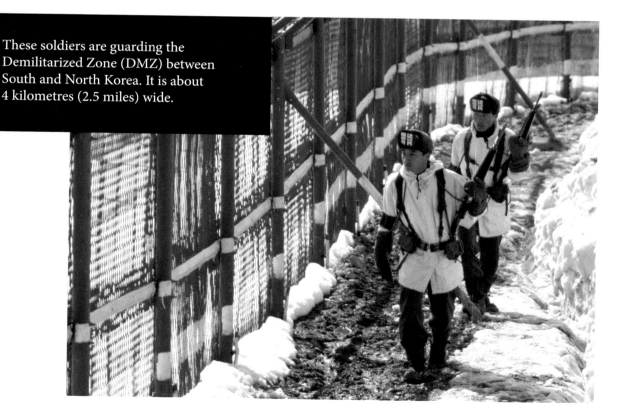

These soldiers are guarding the Demilitarized Zone (DMZ) between South and North Korea. It is about 4 kilometres (2.5 miles) wide.

This family was separated after Korea was divided into two separate countries. They met again in 2010, after 60 years.

South Korea's first presidents were **dictators**. They took away many freedoms from their people. When pupils and workers revolted, they were punished. Gradually, the government changed. Today, South Korea is a strong democracy. It also has a growing **economy**.

Challenge

Peace with the North is South Korea's biggest challenge today. Despite attempts to make peace, the situation remains tense. For example, in March 2010, a South Korean warship sunk, killing 46 South Korean sailors. South Korea blamed North Korea. In November 2010, North Korean troops fired on a South Korean island, killing two marines and two **civilians**. Threats continue. South Korean leaders seek a solution.

Regions and resources: using land wisely

Mountains and rolling hills cover about 70 per cent of South Korea. The Taebaek (also called T'aebaek) Mountain Range is the largest of five ranges. There are four major rivers – the Nakdong, Han, Geum, and Seomjin – and many smaller ones. Many rivers are dry until spring rains fill them. The only natural lake in South Korea is a crater lake at the top of Mount Halla, the highest mountain, located on Jeju (also called Cheju) Island. South Korea has good harbours and popular beaches. There are 3,000 islands, most with no people living on them. However, the largest island, Jeju, has 500,000 people.

Daily Life

Until the 1980s, few South Koreans owned cars. Once they began buying cars, they could drive to South Korea's beautiful beaches. Many beaches have become family resorts. Koreans enjoy swimming, waterskiing, and windsurfing. Snorkelling, surfing, and **parasailing** are also popular.

Beautiful rolling hills cover much of South Korea.

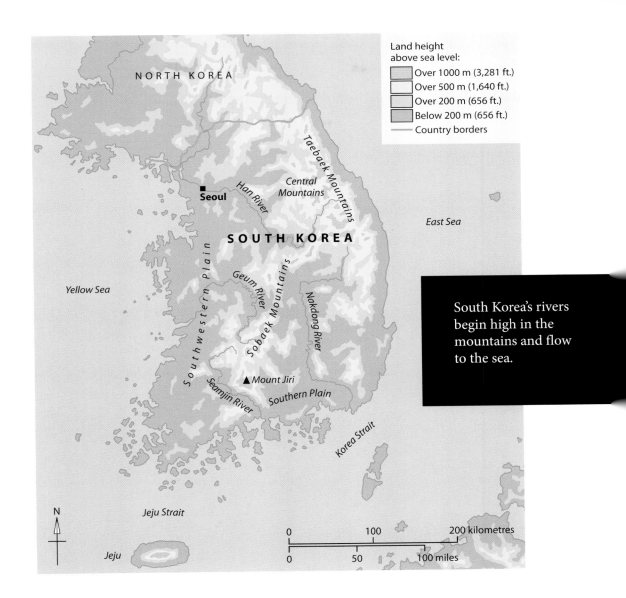

Land height
above sea level:

Over 1000 m (3,281 ft.)
Over 500 m (1,640 ft.)
Over 200 m (656 ft.)
Below 200 m (656 ft.)
Country borders

NORTH KOREA

Seoul

Han River

Central
Mountains

Taebaek Mountains

SOUTH KOREA

East Sea

Southwestern Plain

Geum River

Sobaek Mountains

Nakdong River

Yellow Sea

South Korea's rivers
begin high in the
mountains and flow
to the sea.

Seomjin River

▲ Mount Jiri

Southern Plain

Korea Strait

Jeju Strait

N

Jeju

0   100   200 kilometres

0   50   100 miles

Climate

Korea has four distinct seasons. August is the hottest month. Summers are
rainy, with temperatures that average 26°C (79°F). Winters are cold, with
temperatures just below freezing. It is warmer near the coasts and cooler
further north.

Farming

Most Korean farms are small. However, as young people move to the cities, large company-run farms are becoming more common. Korean farms grow rice, barley, wheat, and a variety of vegetables. Fruit, cotton, tobacco, and **ginseng**, a herb used in medicines, grow well in Korea. Some farmers raise cattle and chickens. South Korea has to **import** food to meet all its needs.

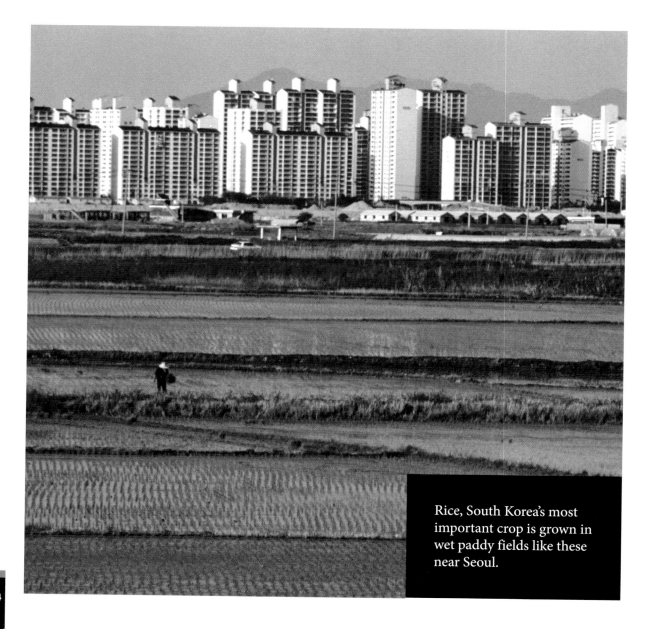

Rice, South Korea's most important crop is grown in wet paddy fields like these near Seoul.

Fishing

Fishing is one of Korea's major **industries**. Anchovy, squid, and mackerel make up half the catch. Yellow croaker and swordfish are important, too. From 1987 to 2000, Korean fishermen **exported** fish to other nations. Beginning in 2001, however, the growing population had to import fish to meet its needs at home.

Industry

About 20 per cent of South Koreans work in **manufacturing** and industry. Coal mining was important before 1990. But as people switched to using oil and new kinds of energy, mining declined. Mines now produce limestone and small amounts of gold, silver, and other minerals.

Korea has many small manufacturing firms producing chemicals, paints, and farm equipment. There are also large family-run businesses, called *jaebeol* (also called *chaebol*). Samsung (electronics), Hyundai (automobiles), and LG (electronics and chemicals) are examples of *jaebeol*. Korea is one of the largest producers of computer chips and of ships.

Wildlife: land of the moon bear

Korea was once home to Siberian tigers, leopards, bears, wolves, and foxes. Today, these animals are rare. Deer, wild boars, rabbits, and badgers still live in the mountains. Korea has about 50 **species** of native birds. About 380 species migrate, or travel, through Korea in the spring and autumn.

YOUNG PEOPLE

Seoul's Children's Grand Park is specially designed for children. There is a zoo which has tigers, elephants, jaguars, meerkats, and penguins. In all, there are 623 animals from 106 different species. The park also includes gardens, a water play area, and amusement rides.

Mountainous National Parks
Marine and Coastal National Parks
Historical National Parks

NORTH KOREA

Seoul

SOUTH KOREA

Mount Jiri

N

| 0 | 100 | 200 kilometres |
| 0 | 50 | 100 miles |

South Korea has fifteen mountain national parks, four marine and coastal national parks, and one historical park.

Environmentalists are trying to save endangered species such as the leopard cat, the Russian rat snake, and the Asiatic black bear (moon bear). Environmentalists had thought moon bears died out – until they discovered six of them in Mt. Jiri (Mt. Chiri) National Park in 2001. They hope to increase the population to 50 by 2012. In the past, moon bears were killed for their meat or used in traditional Chinese medicines.

Plants and flowers

Over 4,500 plant species grow on the Korean **Peninsula**, including the rose, iris, and daisy. **Ginseng** grows wild. The mountains are covered with pine and spruce trees. Maple, oak, elm, and other leaf-bearing trees turn beautiful colours every autumn.

Daily Life

Koreans enjoy hiking in the mountains. National parks include hiking trails. Some are so long that it takes three days to complete the hike. There are campsites and shelters along the way.

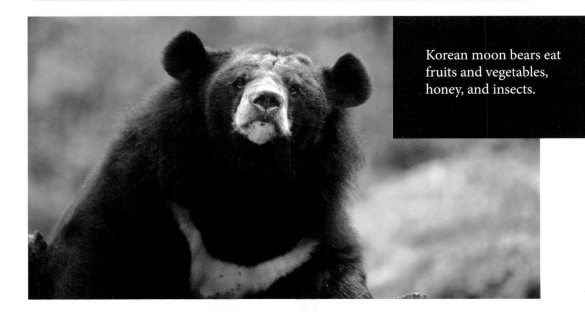

Korean moon bears eat fruits and vegetables, honey, and insects.

Infrastructure: looking to the future

South Korea is a **democracy**. Presidents are elected for a single five-year term. The president appoints a prime minister and other officials. South Korea's first **constitution**, adopted on 17 July 1948, has been rewritten several times. It grants freedom of religion, the right to own property, and the right to vote.

LEE MYUNG-BAK
(BORN 1941)

Lee Myung-bak came from a poor family. He worked his way through university. In 1965 he began working for Hyundai Engineering as a manager. He worked his way up to head the company. In 2002 he became mayor of Seoul. He was elected president of South Korea in 2007.

South Korea's population, life expectancy, population growth, and **median** age have undergone major changes since 1960. Today fewer babies are being born, people are living longer, and the population is growing older.

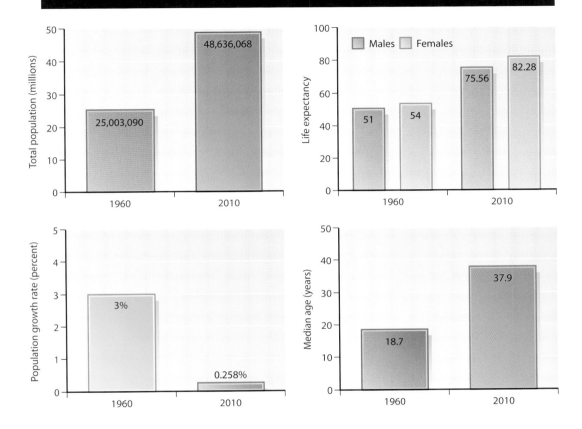

One Korea

The South Korean government has a long-term goal of becoming **unified** with North Korea. Recent South Korean presidents have tried to work with North Korea. In 1998, President Kim Dae-jung introduced the Sunshine Policy, in hopes of establishing peace. Recently, however, North Korea's threats against the South have made it unlikely the two countries will be unified in the near future.

Healthcare

The Ministry of Health and Social Affairs is a government department that supports health programmes throughout South Korea. Nearly everyone has medical insurance. Good medical care helps people live longer. At the same time, people are having fewer children. This means that the population is ageing faster than any other country. An ageing population means fewer workers. It can also mean higher healthcare costs. Older people need more care and require more medicines.

Transport and communication

South Korea has excellent transport and communication systems. Products are shipped all over the world by air and boat. Until recently, car ownership in South Korea was lower than in other Asian nations, but this is changing. Even so, many people use public transport. Underground trains and taxis are available almost everywhere.

BAN KI-MOON (BORN 1944)

Since 2007 the secretary-general of the **United Nations** (**UN**), Ban Ki-moon, has helped to settle conflicts between nations. Before becoming secretary-general, Ban was in charge of South Korea's Ministry of Foreign Affairs and Trade. He speaks Korean, English, and French.

South Korea's Ban Ki-moon is secretary-general of the UN.

YOUNG PEOPLE

All healthy young men are required to serve in the military for about two years after they finish their education. Military service is not required of women. In 2010 about 687,000 soldiers were serving in South Korea's army, navy, and air force.

South Korea has seven radio networks, including **Buddhist**, Christian, and public stations. Over 200 television stations provide news, educational programmes, and entertainment programmes. Many people rely on the Internet and mobile phones. By 2010, South Korea had more mobile phones than people.

Women's roles

Women have the same rights as men in South Korea. Since 2004, 50 per cent of the candidates running for the National Assembly must be women. In 2001 a government department called the Ministry of Gender Equality and Family was established to promote women's rights. Even so, women make only about half as much money as men. Today, many women still face old-fashioned ideas at work or when they run for political office.

These pupils in Daegu use laptop computers instead of textbooks.

Education

South Koreans value education. The **literacy rate** is 97.9 per cent. This means that almost everyone over the age of 15 can read and write. For Korean parents and grandparents, education was the key to a successful future. Today, they push their children to do well in school, too.

Primary school is free. Children begin school at the age of six. Primary school lasts six years, lower secondary school lasts three, and higher secondary school is another three. In primary school, pupils study the Korean language, social studies, mathematics, science, physical education, and fine arts such as music and dance. Pupils begin learning English at the age of eight or nine.

Daily Life

South Korean pupils attend school Monday to Friday and some Saturday mornings. A school day lasts eight hours, and a school year lasts 220 days. That is about 25 days more than most UK school years. Many South Korean pupils also go to private tutors until 10:00 at night to study for university entrance exams.

Pupils must pay to attend secondary school. Many parents choose private schools to give their children a better chance of getting into college or university. Less than half of Korean pupils go to college and university. There are 435 colleges and universities in South Korea.

YOUNG PEOPLE

Many Korean parents send their children to schools in the United Kingdom and the United States. In 2008, 27,350 schoolchildren studied in different countries. University students study abroad, too. In 2009, 113,519 South Korean students attended universities overseas. Only China sends more university pupils overseas.

Culture: meeting of old and new

South Korea's **constitution** grants freedom of religion. Roughly half of South Koreans practise some form of religion. Most believers are Christian (29.2 per cent) or **Buddhist** (22.8 per cent). Some people follow **Islam** or **Judaism**. Many other religious movements exist in this **tolerant** country.

Shamanism, an ancient Korean religion, is still practised by many. Shamanists believe that spirits filled the world. Special people called shamans are thought to communicate with helpful or harmful spirits by chanting and performing special dances.

Confucianism

Confucianism is not a religion. It is a way of thinking that has influenced Korean life for more than 1,000 years. Confucius (551–479 BC) was a Chinese philosopher who developed this belief system to create harmony, or agreement, among people. He taught that people are not equal. For example, parents teach and protect children, while children obey and respect parents. Relationships are about responsibility and respect. Honouring the memory of important **ancestors** is an important part of Confucianism.

Daily Life

Korean is spoken by people in both South Korea and North Korea. The grammar of Korean is similar to Japanese, but about 70 per cent of Korean words come from Chinese.

YOUNG PEOPLE

In South Korea, when a baby is born, he or she is said to be in a first year. But in a new calendar year, a baby is said to enter a second year. For example, a baby born on 15 December is in her first year, but two weeks later, on 1 January, she is said to enter her second year. If asked, her parents would say she is two years old, because she has lived during two different years. This means a child considered to be a 10-year-old in Korea is at least one year younger than a 10-year-old in the United Kingdom.

Koreans wear colourful traditional clothing on New Year's Day and for other special occasions.

Traditional Korean homes are built in an L-shape. Rooms are placed side-by-side along the inside wall, and they open on to a fenced courtyard. The backs of the room form the outside wall of the house. Anyone passing by cannot see into the courtyard. The living space is private. The kitchen is built lower than the other rooms. To provide heat, pipes run from the cooking stove beneath the floor of the house. This system is called *ondol*. It is so popular that even modern city flats have heating pipes beneath the floors.

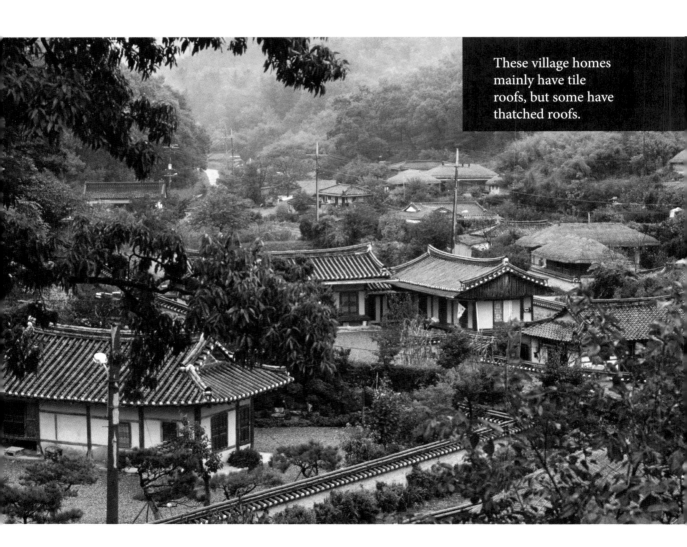

These village homes mainly have tile roofs, but some have thatched roofs.

Daily Life

Koreans never wear shoes in the house. They leave shoes beside the front door. This is because Koreans have clear distinctions between inside and outside. People also spend a lot of time on the floor. They eat at low tables, sitting on the floor, and they sleep on mattresses placed directly on the floor.

Homes

Until the late 1900s, most Koreans lived in farm villages. Children, parents, and grandparents lived together in one home. Today, 81 per cent of the people live in big cities. City dwellers often live in blocks of flats. These flats are often very small, so grandparents live separately.

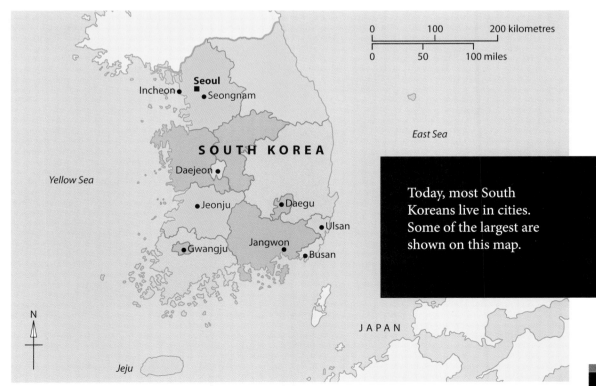

Today, most South Koreans live in cities. Some of the largest are shown on this map.

Music and art

Koreans have a long musical tradition. Ancient music and Korean folk tunes are performed at special concerts. These concerts include some of the 60 musical instruments of ancient Korea. Today, however, most people listen to pop music. South Korean radio stations play jazz, hip-hop, and rap – whatever young people want to hear.

YOUNG PEOPLE

The most popular music today among young South Koreans is K-pop, a kind of pop music often featuring "girl groups". These groups combine simple tunes with rap, an electronic beat, and easy-to-learn dance steps. Groups like Wonder Girls, 2NE1, KARA, After School, and 4Minutes have fans of all ages throughout Asia. Their worldwide audience is growing. Wonder Girls sing their hit "Nobody" in both Korean and English. In 2009 they toured with the Jonas Brothers.

The Wonder Girls, shown here, are one of South Korea's most popular groups.

Ancient art – furniture, metalwork, and pottery – are highly prized today. Art museums throughout the world display Korean art, especially pottery, **calligraphy**, and painting. Modern artists continue to produce works of beauty. Seoul, Busan (also called Pusan), Daegu, and other major cities have art museums open to the public.

Daily Life

The Korean alphabet, called *Hangeul*, has 24 symbols. It was invented in 1446 so that Koreans could learn to read. At the time, educated people wrote Chinese, which has about 6,000 characters. Today, about 1,800 Chinese characters are still in use in Korea, but everyone reads and writes using *Hangeul*.

This 11-year-old girl is practising writing calligraphy.

How to say...

Hello/goodbye   *Annyeong haseyo* (Ahn-nyoung ha-say-yo)

Thank you   *Gamsa hamnida* (Gahm-sa hahm-nida)

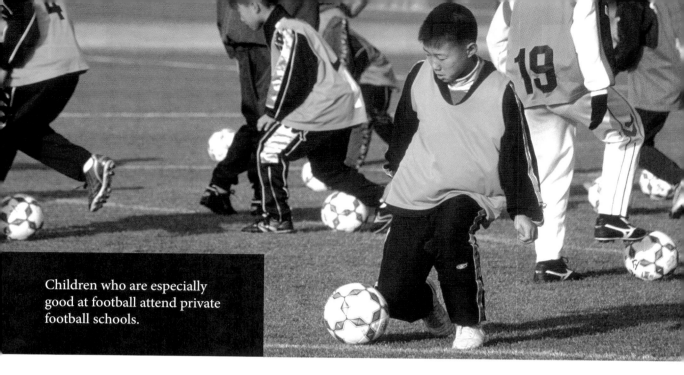

Children who are especially good at football attend private football schools.

Sports

Tae kwon do, a martial art used for self-defence, began in Korea over 2,000 years ago. It is South Korea's national sport. *Ssireum*, which is Korean wrestling, developed 1,500 years ago. Today, national tournaments are held eight times a year. The champion's title is "Strongest Man Under the Heavens".

Football is extremely popular. In 2002 South Korea and Japan hosted the first World Cup held in Asia. They built modern stadiums that are now used by 15 professional teams. Baseball is also popular. Youth football and baseball teams compete internationally. South Korean baseball teams play in the Asia-Pacific Region Little League Championships, competing for a chance to play in the Little League World Series held yearly in Pennsylvania, USA.

The Olympics

South Korea first participated in the 1948 Olympics in London. Since then, South Korean athletes have won 85 gold, 82 silver, and 79 bronze medals. The strongest performances are in speed skating, judo, archery, and wrestling. In 1988 South Korea hosted the Olympics in Seoul. Figure skater Kim Yu-na won gold in the 2010 Olympics held in Vancouver, Canada.

YOUNG PEOPLE

In 2000 the World Cyber Games began in Korea. Nearly one-third of South Koreans play online games called eSports. The most popular is StarCraft, a science fiction game. Major companies such as Samsung and SK Telecom sponsor teams that play in online tournaments. These players, mostly young people, are treated like celebrities. The tournaments are broadcast on television.

Kim Yu-na competed for South Korea in a figure skating competition in Paris in 2009.

Entertainment

People throughout South Korea enjoy films, television, and sporting events. City dwellers enjoy going to the theatre to see plays or operas. Summer sports include hiking, golf, mountain biking, and scuba diving. In winter, people ice skate, ski, and snowboard. There are 14 ski resorts in South Korea, and more are being built.

Foods

Rice is the basis of most Korean meals. *Gimchi* (also called *kimch'i*), a pickled vegetable dish, is made of cabbage with added spices. It is served at most meals, along with rice, soup, and various side dishes. Adding red pepper paste and garlic makes Korean soups and rice hot and spicy. South Koreans eat more garlic per person than people in any other country. The most popular meat dish is *bulgogi* (also called *pulgogi*). It is made of thin strips of lean beef barbecued over hot coals. Fish, pork, and poultry are popular, too.

South Koreans drink tea with their meals. Coffee is also becoming popular. They finish a meal by drinking a broth made from water boiled in the rice pot. They usually eat fruit for dessert.

Daily Life

Koreans do not use forks or knives when eating Korean food. They use spoons for mixing and stirring, and for eating soup and rice. They use chopsticks for meat and side dishes. They rarely eat with their fingers.

Cold cucumber soup

This soup is often eaten on hot summer days. Ask an adult to help you when using the hob or pouring the soup into bowls.

Ingredients

3 small cucumbers, sliced
  matchstick thin
1 teaspoon chilli powder
4 tablespoons cider vinegar
1 tablespoon sugar
2 tablespoons soy sauce

1 tablespoon sesame oil
950 ml water
Ice cubes, for serving
1 tablespoon sesame seeds
  (optional)

What to do

1. In a large bowl, mix the matchstick cucumbers with the chili pepper, vinegar, sugar, soy sauce, and sesame oil.

2. Let the cucumbers sit in the seasoning for 10 minutes.

3. Add water.

4. Chill in the refrigerator.

5. Add sesame seeds and ice cubes before serving.

6. Ladle into individual bowls.

South Korea today

South Korea's greatest challenge today is its relationship with North Korea. Both countries want a **unified** Korea. They share the same history and language. They both value education. However, South Korea is larger, wealthier, and healthier. North Korea has a struggling **economy**, but it has a huge army and **nuclear weapons**. Many South Koreans worry about an attack from the North such as the one that happened in November 2010.

The future

Despite this overwhelming challenge, South Korea is moving boldly into the future. South Korea has good relations with many other countries, a strong economy, and an excellent communication system. Like China, India, and Japan, South Korea has entered the space race. In August 2009 and June 2010, South Korean scientists attempted to launch satellites into space. Both launches failed, but South Korea's space programme will continue. South Koreans have always worked hard to reach their goals.

Comparing North and South Korea

	South Korea	North Korea
Population	48,754,657 (2011 est.)	24,457,492 (2011 est.)
Government	**Democracy**	**Communist** dictatorship
Per capita income (average money earned in each household)	£17,800 (2009 est.)	£1,100 (2009 est.)
Life expectancy	79.05 years (2011 est.)	68.89 years (2011 est.)
Telephones	19.29 million (2009)	1.18 million (2008)
Nuclear weapons	No	Yes

Since 1948, the two Koreas have made different choices.

Daily Life

South Koreans and North Koreans speak the same language. However, the dialect (local version of the language) spoken in the South is *Hangugeo* (also called *Han'gugo*). In North Korea the dialect is called *Joseonmal* (also called *Chosonmal*). People can usually understand one another, but they spell words differently.

Schoolchildren in Goheung, near the Naro Space Center, cheer for the 2010 rocket launch.

YOUNG PEOPLE

On the first anniversary of a child's birth, families celebrate with a look into the future. The child is given a choice of several items that may predict his or her future. A gold coin means wealth. A pen means life as a writer. A piece of thread means long life. A book means life as a scholar.

Fact file

Official name:	**Republic** of Korea
Nationality:	Korean
Official language:	Korean
Capital city:	Seoul
Bordering countries:	North Korea to the north
Population:	48,754,657 (July 2011 est.)
Largest cities (populations):	Seoul (10.5 million) Busan (3.6 million) Incheon (2.7 million) (part of Seoul metropolitan area) Daegu (2.5 million)
System of government:	Republic
Date of independence:	15 August 1945 (from Japan)
Date of constitution:	Current **constitution** approved on 29 October 1987
Religion:	Christian (29.2 per cent), **Buddhist** (22.8 per cent), none (46.5 per cent)
Life expectancy:	79.05 years (2011 est.)
Literacy rate:	97.9 per cent
Climate:	Moderate temperatures, with four seasons

Area (total):	99,720 square kilometres (38,502 square miles)
Coastline:	2,413 kilometres (1,499 miles)
Longest river:	Nakdong, 521 kilometres (324 miles)
Highest elevation:	Mount Halla, 1,950 metres (6,398 feet)
Lowest elevation:	East Sea, 0 metres (0 feet)
Local currency:	Won (₩)
Agriculture products:	Rice, root crops, barley, vegetables, fruits; cattle, pigs, chickens, milk, eggs; fish
Major industries:	Electronics, telecommunications, automobile production, chemicals, shipbuilding, steel
Imports:	Machinery, electronics and electronic equipment, oil, steel, transport equipment, organic chemicals, plastics
Exports:	Semi-conductors, wireless telecommunications equipment, motor vehicles, computers, steel, ships, chemical products
Major markets:	China (21.5 per cent), United States (10.9 per cent), Japan (6.6 per cent), Hong Kong (4.6 per cent) (2008)
Major suppliers:	China (17.7 per cent), Japan (14 per cent), United States (8.9 per cent), Saudi Arabia (7.8 per cent), United Arab Emirates (4.4 per cent), Australia (4.1 per cent) (2008)

National flower: *Mugunghwa* (Rose of Sharon)

National coat of arms: Adopted in 1963, it features a symbol called *taeguk*
bordered by five petals and a ribbon bearing the inscription
"The Republic of Korea" in *Hangeul* characters. The *taeguk*
can also be seen on the flag on page 46.

Famous South Koreans: Ban Ki-moon (born 1944), secretary-general of the **UN**
Kim Dae-jung (born 1925), president of South Korea,
   winner of 2000 Nobel Peace Prize for efforts to achieve
   peace with North Korea
Kim Yu-na (born 1990) 2010 Olympic gold medal ice skater
Moon Dae-sung (born 1976) 2004 Olympic gold medallist
   in **tae kwon do**
Park Ji-Sung (born 1981) footballer who plays for
   Manchester United
Rain (born 1982) pop singer

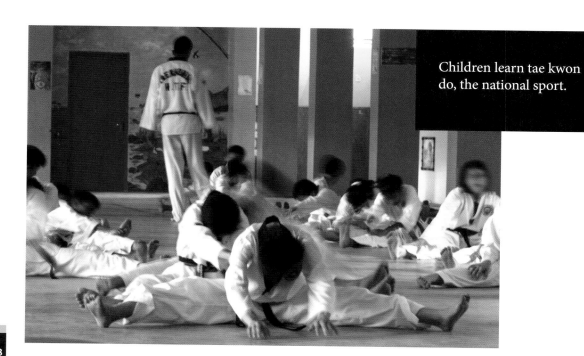

Children learn tae kwon do, the national sport.

National holidays:

1 January	New Year's Day
Lunar calendar New Year (1st day of 1st month)	Seolla
1 March	Independence Movement Day
5 May	Children's Day
Lunar calendar (8th day of 4th month)	Buddha's Birthday
6 June	Memorial Day
15 August	Liberation Day
Lunar calendar (15th day of 8th month)	Chuseok (Harvest Festival)
3 October	National Foundation Day
25 December	Christmas

National anthem
"Aegukga" ("Love the Country")

Rose of Sharon, thousand miles of range and river land! Guarded by her people, ever may Korea stand!

Until the East Sea's waves are dry, (and) Mt. Baektusan worn away, God watch o'er our land forever! Our Korea manse!

Like that Mt. Namsan armoured pine, standing on duty still, wind or frost, unchanging ever, be our resolute will.

In autumn's arching evening sky, crystal, and cloudless blue, Be the radiant moon our spirit, steadfast, single, and true.

With such a will, (and) such a spirit, loyalty, heart and hand, Let us love, come grief, come gladness, this, our beloved land!

Timeline

BC is short for "Before Christ". BC is added after a date and means that the date occurred before the birth of Jesus Christ, for example, 450 BC.

AD is short for *Anno Domini*, which is Latin for "in the year of our Lord". AD is added before a date and means that the date occurred after the birth of Jesus Christ, for example, AD 720.

BC

28,000	Ancient people live on the Korean **Peninsula**.
3000	**Ancestors** of modern Korean people move to the Korean Peninsula from Asia.
2333	Dangun founds the Old Joseon Kingdom.
108	China conquers the northern part of Korea.
57	The kingdoms of Goguryeo, Silla, and Baekje are formed.

AD

300s	The Goguryeo Kingdom becomes **Buddhist**.
668	Korea becomes **unified** under the Silla Kingdom.
935	Wang Geon, the founder of the Goryeo **Dynasty**, rules Korea.
1231	Mongols invade Korea.
1392	Yi Seonggye, the founder of the new Joseon Dynasty, becomes ruler.
1446	The Korean alphabet is invented.
1600s	Manchurians invade Korea.
1876	Japan forces Korea to become a trading partner.
1910	Japan claims Korea as a **colony**.

1945   Korea is divided into two separate territories. The United States oversees South Korea, while the **Soviet Union** oversees North Korea.

1950–1953   North Korea invades South Korea. The **UN** sends troops to assist South Korea. A truce (agreement) is declared in 1953.

1988   Seoul hosts the Summer Olympics.

1998   President Kim Dae-jung begins the Sunshine Policy to encourage open relations with North Korea.

2000   President Kim Dae-jung meets with North Korean President Kim Jong Il in Pyongyang, the capital of North Korea. This is the first meeting between the two countries in 55 years.

2000   President Kim Dae-jung becomes the first South Korean to win the Nobel Peace Prize.

2002   South Korea hosts the World Cup.

2007   South Korea's foreign minister, Ban Ki-moon, becomes secretary general of the UN; Korea elects Lee Myung-bak as its tenth president.

2008   President Lee announces a new environmentally friendly policy.

2010   Seoul is named the 2010 World Design Capital, based on its use of architecture to improve city life.

Glossary

ancestor person from whom an individual is descended; someone more distant than a grandparent

artificial human-made; not natural

Buddhist of the religion Buddhism, originated in India by Buddha (Siddhartha Gautama)

calligraphy highly decorative handwriting

civilian person who is not a member of the military

colony area ruled by another country

communist person or country that practises a social system in which all people share work and property

constitution system of laws and principles that govern a nation, state, or corporation

culture practices, beliefs, and traditions of a society

Demilitarized Zone (DMZ) artificial boundary between North and South Korea about 4 kilometres (2.5 miles) wide, designed to keep their fighting forces separated

democracy form of government made up of members who have been chosen by the people of the country

dictator ruler with absolute power over the people

dolmen kind of burial tomb

dynasty series of rulers from the same family or group

economy having to do with the money, industries, and jobs in a country

endangered at risk of being completely killed off

environmentalist someone who works to protect the air, water, animals, plants, and other natural resources from pollution or its effects

export to ship goods to other countries for sale or exchange

ginseng herb used in medicine

import to bring in from a foreign country for use or sale

industry general business activity or trade

Islam religion founded in Saudi Arabia during the AD 600s based on the teachings of Muhammad

Judaism religion that began among ancient Hebrews. They believe in one god.

literacy rate number of people over the age of 15 who can read and write

manufacturing making or producing a product by hand or machinery

median middle value in a set of data

nuclear weapon missile or bomb that uses energy made by splitting atoms

parasailing sport of soaring in a parachute while being pulled along, usually by a motorboat

peninsula land area almost completely surrounded by water and connected to the mainland by a narrow strip of land

republic independent country with a head of government who is not a king or queen

shrine sacred or holy place

Soviet Union former union of 15 republics in Eastern Europe and Asia that ended in 1991

species particular type of animal or plant

tae kwon do Korean martial art used in self-defence

tolerant able to accept the beliefs or opinions of others

unify make into a single unit

United Nations (UN) international organization formed in 1945 to promote world peace

Find out more

Books

Countries of the World: South Korea, Tom Jackson (National Geographic Society, 2007)

Countries of the World: South Korea, Rob Bowden (Evans Brothers, 2005)

Our World Divided: North and South Korea, Cath Senker (Wayland, 2011)

The Atlas of People and Places, Philip Steele (Franklin Watts, 2008)

The Usborne Geography Encyclopedia, Jane Bingham et al (Usborne, 2010)

Websites

https://www.cia.gov/library/publications/the-world-factbook/index.html

The World Factbook provides information on the history, people, government, geography, and more of South Korea and over 250 other nations.

http://english.visitkorea.or.kr/enu/index.kto

To plan a trip to Korea – real or imaginary – visit Korea's official tourism website.

www.timeforkids.com/TFK/kids/hh/goplaces/main/0,28375,927166,00.html

Learn more about South Korea at Time for Kids.

http://kids.nationalgeographic.com/kids/places/find/south-korea/

Watch a video about the women divers of South Korea's Jeju Island on the National Geographic website.

http://news.bbc.co.uk/2/hi/asia-pacific/country_profiles/1123668.stm

Find out about South Korea on the BBC's website.

http://whc.unesco.org/en/list

This page on the UNESCO website provides a list of all the World Heritage sites in South Korea and the rest of the world.

Places to visit

If you are lucky enough to visit South Korea, here are some of the places you could visit:

Children's Grand Park, Seoul
The Children's Grand Park includes a zoo, gardens, a playground, and an amusement park designed especially for children.

Gyeongju historic sites
Learn about the ancient Silla Dynasty in the city of Gyeongju by visiting ancient shrines, temples, and the Gyeongju National Museum. This city is about an hour north of Busan.

Mt. Sorak National Park
This large national park is located on the northeastern coast of South Korea along the East Sea. Hiking trails lead up Mt. Sorak, the second highest mountain on mainland South Korea with an elevation over 1,524 metres (5,000 feet). Hike up to the Bronze Buddha statue or visit the tall waterfalls along the Flying Dragon trail.

Jeju Island
Visit the Jeju Folk Museum or the Seongeup Folk Village on South Korea's largest island.

Topic tools

You can use these topic tools for your school projects. Trace the flag and map on to a sheet of paper, using the thick black outlines to guide you. Then colour in your pictures. Make sure you use the right colours for the flag!

The South Korean flag, called the *taegeukgi*, has three parts. There's a white background. White is the traditional colour of the Korean people. In the centre is a red and blue yin-yang symbol. It stands for unity. The four black symbols in the corners represent heaven, moon, sun, and earth. The flag was adopted in 1882.

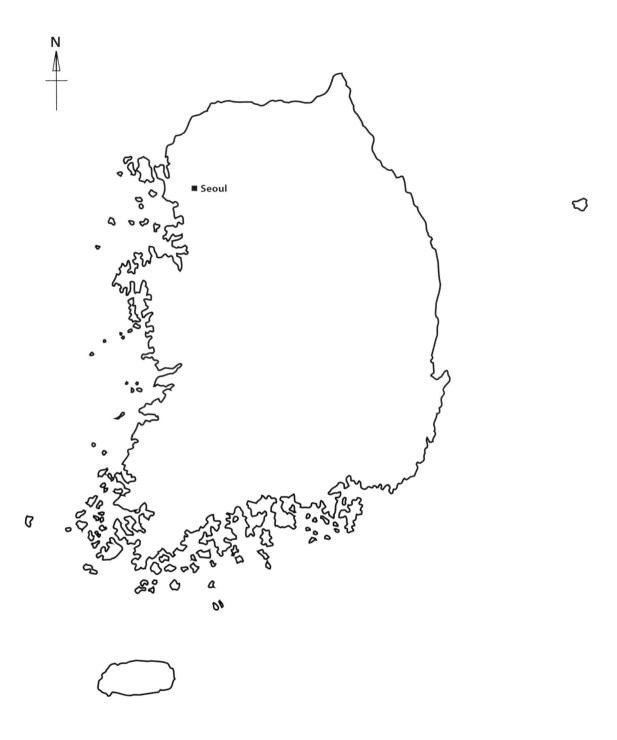

N

■ Seoul

Index

Titles in the series